Ruth and Boo

By Carmel Reilly

Contents

Home on the Farm

This big farm is Ruth's home.

Her mum and dad grow fruit on the farm.

Ruth has a lot of pets.

She has one dog, two cats and many hens!

But she loves Boo the most.

Boo is her new pony.

Week Days

Ruth gets up at six
on week days.

She runs out to see Boo
before school.

Boo neighs at Ruth
to say hi!

Ruth drops a few scoops
of food into Boo's tub.

Ruth gets back home
from school at five.

She zooms out to see Boo.

Ruth rubs Boo's back and neck.

She feeds Boo some fruit
that grew on the farm.

Weekends

On the weekend, Ruth likes to groom Boo.

First, she cleans dirt from Boo's hooves.

Then, she checks Boo's coat.

She grooms his mane and tail.

Next, Ruth puts on her boots.

She sets Boo up for a ride.

Boo and Ruth zoom down
the farm track.

Then, Boo and Ruth go
to the pool.

At the pool, Boo gets
a cool drink.

Ruth brings Boo back
to the barn.

She grooms Boo and takes
him outside.

Ruth sweeps out Boo's bed with a broom.

She puts down fresh hay.

Ruth and Boo have had a great day!

CHECKING FOR MEANING

1. Other than Boo, what pets does Ruth have? *(Literal)*

2. What does Ruth do to groom Boo? *(Literal)*

3. What does Ruth do to show how much she loves Boo? *(Inferential)*

EXTENDING VOCABULARY

scoops	What are *scoops*? How much food is in a scoop? Are all scoops the same size?
groom	What does *groom* mean in this text? Is there another meaning of this word? At a wedding, who is the groom?
hooves	What are *hooves*? Does the word *hooves* mean one or more than one? What is the singular form of this word?

MOVING BEYOND THE TEXT

1. Do you have pets? What are they? If not, what pets would you like to have?

2. How do you care for your pet? What does your pet eat? Do you have to bath your pet? Have you ever taken your pet to the vet? Why?

3. Talk about which pets are easy to care for and which pets require more time to look after them.

4. Make a list of things your parents may talk to you about before you get a new pet.

SPEED SOUNDS

oo	ue	ew	ui	u_e

ou	u	oe	o

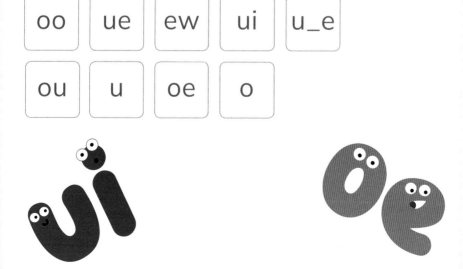

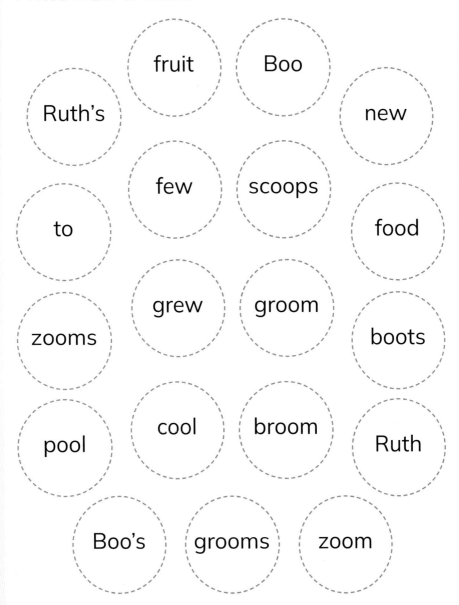

fruit

Boo

Ruth's

new

few

scoops

to

food

grew

groom

zooms

boots

pool

cool

broom

Ruth

Boo's

grooms

zoom